SPECTRUM®
READERS

AMAZING!
Structures

By Katharine Kenah

Carson-Dellosa
Publishing

SPECTRUM®

An imprint of Carson-Dellosa Publishing, LLC
P.O. Box 35665
Greensboro, NC 27425-5665

carsondellosa.com

Printed in the USA. All rights reserved.
ISBN 978-1-62399-141-8

01-002131120

There are many amazing creations
on earth.
Some of these creations are man–made.
Thousands of people visit these places
every year.
Have you seen any of these
amazing creations?

Stonehenge

Look at what is in England!
Stonehenge is a very old creation.
It is made of huge stones.
The stones form circles.
Some people think that Stonehenge
was a kind of church.

Pyramid and Great Sphinx

Look at what is in Egypt!
People built this pyramid
over 4,000 years ago.
It is made of thousands of stone blocks.
The blocks are as big and heavy
as trucks.
The Great Sphinx is also very old.
It has the face of a man and the body
of a lion.

Great Wall of China

Look at what is in China!
The Great Wall of China
is the longest creation on earth.
It is about 4,000 miles long.
The wall is so long that it can be seen
from outer space!

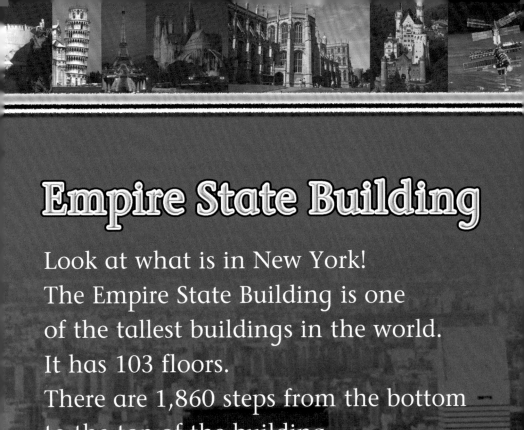

Empire State Building

Look at what is in New York!
The Empire State Building is one
of the tallest buildings in the world.
It has 103 floors.
There are 1,860 steps from the bottom
to the top of the building.

Mount Rushmore

Look at what is in South Dakota!
Mount Rushmore is a sculpture
of four American presidents.
Their faces are cut into the side
of a cliff.
It took over ten years to carve
the faces out of the rock!

Golden Gate Bridge

Look at what is in California!
The Golden Gate Bridge is one
of the largest bridges in the world.
It crosses part of the San Francisco Bay.
The Golden Gate Bridge is not gold.
It is really orange!

The White House

Look at what is in Washington, D.C.!
The White House is the home
of the President of the United States.
It has 132 rooms and 35 bathrooms.
The President works on the first floor.
The President's family lives
on the second floor.

Hoover Dam

Look at what is between Nevada
and Arizona!
The Hoover Dam is a huge, high wall.
It is as tall as a 70-story building.
The Hoover Dam crosses
the Colorado River.
Water flows through the dam
and runs machines that make electricity.

Leaning Tower of Pisa

Look at what is in Italy!
The Tower of Pisa is a bell tower.
It is nearly 1,000 years old.
After the Tower of Pisa was built,
it started to tip over.
That was because the ground under it
was soft.
Scientists found ways to keep it
from falling.

Eiffel Tower

Look at what is in Paris, France!
The Eiffel Tower was built
for the World's Fair in 1889.
It is 986 feet tall.
This is about as tall as 170 people!
The tower is made of iron and steel.

Notre Dame

Look at what else is in Paris, France!
Notre Dame is a large, famous church.
It has three big rose windows.
The windows are made of colored glass
and shaped like roses.
Stone animals, called *gargoyles*,
line the edges of the roof.

Windsor Castle

Look at what is close to London!
Windsor Castle is home
to the kings and queens of England.
The castle covers as much ground
as nine football fields.
When the queen is at home,
a special flag flies above the castle.

Neuschwanstein Castle

Look at what is in Germany!
Neuschwanstein Castle was built
for King Ludwig of Bavaria
over 150 years ago.
The castle had running water, toilets,
heat, and bathtubs.
This castle was the model for the
Sleeping Beauty Castle at Disneyland®!

International Space Station

Look at what is in outer space!
Many astronauts and scientists
work inside the space station.
They live there and study outer space.
The space station goes around the earth
one time every 92 minutes.

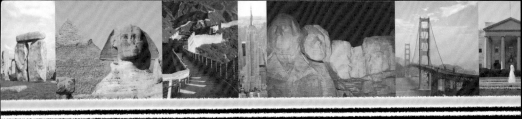

AMAZING! Structures Comprehension Questions

1. What is Stonehenge made from?

2. How old is the pyramid in Egypt? Do you think it was easy or hard to build?

3. How long is the Great Wall of China?

4. How many steps does the Empire State Building have?

5. Describe Mount Rushmore. Can you name one president who is a part of the sculpture?

6. Where is the Golden Gate Bridge? Why do you think the bridge is famous?

7. Who lives in the White House? Why do you think it is called the White House?

8. What river does the Hoover Dam cross?